Distance

Tan-Ku Sequences & Sets

Mariko Kitakubo and Deborah P Kolodji

Distance
Tan-Ku Sequences & Sets

ISBN: 978-1-7377113-6-0

Library of Congress Control Number: 2023932505

Shabda Press
Duarte, California
www.shabdapress.com

Contents

we hold virtual hands

the eternal wind

I slow down to breathe

the traces of us

a city's landmarks

as the road bends

my words drift

Our Tan-Ku Journey

It's 4:30 a.m. in Los Angeles and I'm in the hospital for overnight observation. A nurse comes in to check my vitals and I'm wide awake, in an unfamiliar room. Everyone I know must be sound asleep. Then, I realize that it's early evening in Tokyo, so I message Mariko, "lab specimen/the bar codes/on my wrist band."

She messages me back, "You're up early!" Then, she types, "open to/escape from/the research unit.../waterfall sounds/washing my ears." I think of my IV and grin. A new Tan-Ku set is born.

Or, one afternoon while sipping tea in my patio, my phone beeps with a message from Mariko.

"I'm sipping breakfast tea in my patio" and she sends me a photo. I send her a photo back and then the Tan-Ku sequence, "Both Sides of the Ocean," starts tumbling out.

Writing these poems of tanka/haiku response occurred organically, it wasn't something we set out to create. After a busy poetry travel year in 2019, where Mariko travelled to Los Angeles to do a tanka reading and I travelled to Tokyo to do a presentation at an English language haiku conference, all travel ceased due to the pandemic.

Mariko has been a tanka ambassador for 18 years, performing bilingual tanka readings in 54 different cities, 12 different countries, and on 5 different continents. I have moderated the local Southern California Haiku Study Group with monthly workshops for over 15 years, travelling annually to various haiku conferences. Then came this time, when everything just stopped. Live poetry readings, workshops, and conferences ceased and everyone became isolated. Out of this isolation and distance, Mariko and I started having tanka/haiku conversations and found it addicting, the differences between tanka and haiku expressed as two voices, complementing each other. It kept us connected, sometimes writing at odd hours due to the time difference, but no longer so isolated. Since our first collaboration in 2020, we've written 90 of these poems so far.

At some point, saying tanka/haiku sequences and tanka/haiku sets seemed clumsy, and we felt they needed a name. So, we started calling them Tan-Ku.

All of the tanka in these poems were written by Mariko and all of the haiku in these poems were written by me. The italics refer only to the second voice in the poem, not particularly to either one of us, since some of our Tan-Ku start with a tanka but others start with a haiku. But we like the look of italics for the second voice in each poem.

I'd like to thank Mariko for being my writing partner and becoming like a long-lost sister on the other side of the world that I didn't even know I had. We'd both like to thank Clayton Beach for publishing our first collaboration in *Under the Basho* and his support of this form of collaborative writing, and most of all to Chúc Mỹ Tuệ for believing in our work and publishing this book.

I hope you enjoy this poetic journey as much as we enjoyed writing it.

Deborah P Kolodji

Gratitude for Tan-Ku

I met Deborah, a dear friend of mine, a talented writer and a well-known poet, at a haiku conference at the Asilomar conference facility on the Monterey Peninsula in California, USA, in 2007.

She told me that she was impressed by my tanka reading performance, and since then, we quickly became close friends.

How encouraging our friendship has been to me in the wake of the Covid-19 disaster, when we suddenly lost our yearly routine of traveling back and forth between our countries and seeing each other every year without fail.

The many co-creations we spun together, exchanging daily via smartphone messages were like a stream flowing in the light and shade.

If there is one thing that the pandemic has given us, I would say it is "Tan-Ku," a string of words from our souls uttered while gritting our teeth and overcoming hardships.

I express my heartfelt thanks to Deborah for walking with me despite the physical distance and time difference between us.

I would also like to thank Chúc Mỹ Tuệ of Shabda Press for making my dream of publication come true.

Mariko Kitakubo
https://www.en.kitakubo.com

文学者、表現者、そして人間的にも尊敬する友、Deborah氏 に出会ったのは、2007年アメリカ、カリフォルニア州モントレー半島の施設Asilomarで行われた俳句イベントでした。

私の短歌朗読パフォーマンスに感動して下さった彼女とは、すぐに親しくなりました。

其々の国を行き来し、毎年必ず顔を合わせる日常が急に失われた2020年以降は、文字通り友情に支えられ、生きる望みを繋いだ日々でした。

スマートフォンのメッセージで交流しながら紡いだ共作の数々が、まるで照り陰りながら流れるせせらぎのように、互いの心を潤しました。

パンデミックがただ一つ私達に与えてくれたことがあるとすれば、それは無我夢中で不安を乗り越えながら発した魂の言葉のつらなり、*"Tan-Ku"ではないでしょうか。

物理的距離と時差に隔てられながらも、ともに歩んで下さったDeborah氏へ、心からの感謝を捧げます。

そして今回、出版の夢を叶えて下さっだShabda Press のChúc Mỹ Tuệ 氏にも、深く御礼申し上げます。

どうもありがとうございました。

北久保まりこ

*"Tan-Ku"　Deborah P Kolodji氏と共に編み出した詩歌文学のジャンル。短歌と俳句（又は俳句と短歌）が交互に編まれる。短歌・俳句がそれぞれ二作品以上の場合をTan-Ku Sequence（Tan-Ku連作）、一作品ずつの場合をTan-Ku Set（Tan-Kuセット）と呼び、どちらも題名を伴った形で完結する。

we hold virtual hands

Distance 2020

ruins
of Tokyo appear
in my dream . . .
a storm coming through
verdant freshness

heat lightning
the faces of those
I love

searching
for my favorite
earring . . .
voices in
an empty shell

volunteer tomatoes
the way my life
used to be

sun whispers
to my wings
where
is the rainbow
after green showers

darker skies
and yet . . . tadpoles
in the puddles

handful
of unfinished lives
we were
born from water
undying melody

distant galaxies
the infinite music
of stars

a comet
brought me
the memory
of blue inlet
before my birth

shaky first steps
          a baby's
mine after surgery

when and
how many times
reborn anew
swimming
in the Milky Way

a ray of dawn
across my pillow. . .
birdsong

after
the long darkness
prayers
are falling—
resurrection horizon

empty churches
we hold virtual hands
in online meetings

Circling the Sun

waving
and calming
each other
rondo round
merry-go-round

calliope echoes
a little boy's hand
now larger in mine

August Morning

bees in soft petals
I open my arms
to the sun

overwhelmed
by the damask rose
garden
I'm 62. . .
but a woman yet

Tilt of the Earth

2 am silence
my longing for another
time zone

am I
the sleeping baby
in the womb. . .
tilt
of the earth axis

dawn's first steps
the length
of a day

fly along
the midnight
sky
I will be waiting
under a lotus leaf

setting sun
a white ibis forages
in the tidal basin

ebb and flow. . .
the ancient rhythm
of our cradles
as we search the beach
on the moon

the earth spins
a little girl twirls
her skirt

quiet
tsukimi season
finding
the purple moon
in a puddle

Dream Traveler

moonbeams
my thoughts beyond
this bed

large arc
of the crater
in Tanzania
I am a fragile species
homo sapiens

lights line the path
past sleeping passengers
evening flight

watching
midsummer
splash—
dreamy travel
for a light year

gamma-ray burst
the collapse of a star
we've never heard of

endless. . .
the old melody
countless
golden bubbles
in the spiral galaxy

Ebb and Flow

dreaming to return
to ancestral seas
the pendulum
keeps moving
possible impossible. . .

Foucault thoughts
swing in all directions
the earth turns

Both Sides of the Ocean

tea for both
sides of the ocean
smiling moon

sharing
time under
the big dipper—
gentle roundness
of our horizon

was it only yesterday?
cherry blossoms line
a graveyard

chatting
on the terrace. . .
our roses
under my sun
under your moon

I look up
through bougainvillea
skies we once traveled

clouds come
into my tea cup
and go out. . .
do they drift
from mine to yours?

Connecting Souls

there is
an invisible thread
between us. . .
quietness of
the pearl oyster

closing my eyes
I see your face
Vermeer's earring

Vertigo

chilly morning
a white moth
is resting
out of my window
out of my inner chaos

unsteady walk
through the garden
buzzing world

the eternal wind

Epochs

calmed by
the rhythm of tides
my stress

inner song
we can go back
anytime
fetal movement of
the Cambrian ocean

trilobite seas
our understanding
evolves

get lost
in the Stromatlite
lagoon
peppermint blue moon
of 35 billion years ago

the world
a simpler place
time travel dreams

an ammonite
in the city wall
watching
the eternal wind
Mare Adriatico

University Hospital

lab specimen
the bar codes
on my wrist band

open to
escape from
the research unit. . .
waterfall sounds
washing my ears

Resolve

the purpose
of my life has changed
again. . .
focus on the lady
in the full-length mirror

morning sun comes
through the window
I stand taller

Illness

high waves
of uselessness
my hands
can't swim across
the ocean to help you

sunrise glow
an encouraging text
from another time zone

dawn of
golden ripples
moonrise
of silver dune
sharing our star

spent daffodils
the feeling of being
dormant

sharp
angle of a sundial
searching
the other side
of the Universe

a meteor
flashes the sky
hope for a cure

Emergence

hearing
the first cicada
in Tokyo
he fights the virus
in his small body

train station
the air soup between
our masks

This Time Apart

may I
breathe, think
or love
this time apart
in a PET scan

flat on my back
into the tunnel
flashing lights

my eyes
cannot see
inside of me. . .
where is my love
where is yours

iodine veins
thoughts spinning around
my head

a dream
for a few seconds
I am
embraced by
the dark universe

night deepens
that moment when
the stars come out

Cancer

wind will bring
the summer storm...
my garden
bordered by living
cadmium yellow

wild mustard
growing out of control
clinical trial

To Fly Without Fear

the lonely cry
of a red-crowned crane
patio tea break

may I be me?
can I be me,
I should be me
did somebody see me?
I am here without my name

no visitors
in the COVID wing
hospital wrist band

humming
of angel wings
I dream
in the sickroom
your footsteps

green canopy
I walk the forest
of my mind

call me
by our secret
word
to be able to fly
without fear

Motherless

a lavender
bubble bath makes me
remember
the shades of
mum's yukata

combing out my hair
I close my eyes
and see her face

Autumn Ghosts

standing alone
with my thoughts
my birth
and Mother's death
fall rain

clearing her house
a faded pink
baby blanket

wearing
her kimono
suddenly
I meet her
in my shadow

daughter's wedding
the sparkle
of my mother's rings

sounds
of Autumn steps,
not only mine
on the leaves. . .
calm colors of earth

soulful eyes
inheriting
a dog

Songs in White

the melody
of text messages
winter isolation

I try to escape
from the underlying loss. . .
the music box still
there
since childhood

I slow down to breathe

Forest Bathing

uphill path
I slow down to breathe
the pine scent

she perches
at the edge of
my straw hat
a butterfly's siesta
in emerald breeze

Under the Sun

early heat wave
the shade tree not yet
leafed out

road mirage,
the wait for thunder--
ordering
a scoop of pistachio
ice cream

earth baked
by relentless sun
my wide-brimmed hat

high tide
tomorrow always
comes
the shiny edge
of the field of vision

aloe vera
the cool rub down after
a heated argument

the thorns
were young green
never-ending
vacation
in Mallorca

Beach in Malaysia

grey skies
the blues inside
me

running
through rainforest
to the cove
accompanied by lightning
and a rainbow

Music of the Galaxy

twin firefly
between the air
and reflection
on the lake
Claire de Lune

early morning birth
Perseid fireworks
light up the sky

joining you
with Orionid showers
our story
has begun
great symphony

dark skies
a sonata of stars
away from the city

alone
the silhouette
of the galaxy
hearing the music
thousands of strings

my heart
open to the heavens
stargazer lily

Parthenon Wind

swinging
a velvet seed pod
between
Heraclitus and
Parmenides

a new nest
in the wisteria frame
the same doves again

Seedlings

delicate sounds
of the early spring
taking time
to melt the waterfall
shining in the sun

sound of rain
outside my bedroom
morning lullaby

soft drops
of humidity
in Tokyo
no one notices
my tears

shall I go. . .
        shall I stay?
the absence of thunder

pouring
your favorite
blueberry tea
under the stars
scent of firewood

cloudless skies
seedlings after
last year's ashes

Sirius Rising

dog days
my maltipoo and I
stay inside and sleep

the joy
of getting lost. . .
am I in
the sky or ocean?
lapis lazuli

Beach House

the iridescent
splash still there
after your dive. . .
eternal summer
eternal ocean

the sea pounding
even in my dreams
dolphins

The Course of Water

drip drip drip
from an IV bag
dreams of mountain streams

midnight river
calls her love...
the carved
wood dragon is wet
in the morning

legends of the heart
the old well my mother
drew from

the fossil
from the depth
of Sahara,
tell me your story
a shell holds the cavity

where water gushed
our footprints
in dry sand

a fountain
appears in blue. . .
we were born
from aqua, too
Samarkand

After Sunset

you are
at the beach
tonight. . .
searching a shell in Tokyo
to hear a distant roar

moonlight
on the water
neap tide

Time

sea breeze
those younger versions
of us

sandy trail
to the beach
everything
was young including
our dreams

sea thrift
on coastal cliffs
memory erosion

the natural
healing power
was given
to my toes,
endless waves

pelicans dive
the many songs
of ocean

lives
wake from
the depth
sea glass
in the memorial inlet

Footsteps

autumn forest
deepens and deepens
in color
who knows
when I will disappear

chilled by the wind
each step closer
to winter

the traces of us

In the Wind

wild dogs
can smell
our wildness
the traces of us
in ruined cities

a mockingbird
learns a new song
refugees

it might
be raining ashes
across the sea
across the border
settled in time

wings of planes
wings of birds
no doves

waiting
for a twig of
olive
shining green
forgotten ark

new skies
condors return
from near-extinction

Forecast

early twilight
the angry voices
next door

darkness is hiding
under children's brims
tomorrow
will be a sunny day. . .
after the war

Stormy

spring snow
or petals of sakura
falling falling
like ashes
in Ukraine

trains going west
a child's stuffed bear
stares out the window

whose uniform. . .
a sunflower sprout
comes out
of the camouflage
pocket

the caws of crows
footage of survivors
underground

searching for
better days...
repeated invasions
in our layered
past

petal storm
is there a chance
for peace

Hanging Overhead

in the heat
of all this anger
an umbrella

round shade
makes me calm
even if
nuclear light can
penetrate this thin film

End of the Tunnel

no one knows. . .
I escaped from
his violence
silent night
holy night

no more scarves
to hide the bruises
New Year's resolution

Storm Watch

midsummer heat
the breeze from the fan
not enough

lightning
kisses with
open sea. . .
typhoon from
offshore Thailand

Unexpected Transplant

far from home
the wistful warble
of a red-whiskered bulbul

carefree
in the treetops
singing
iiyoiiyo
iiyoiiyo

across the ocean. . .
do the other birds
hear his call

rainforest
ancestral love
in Asia
green shower
carols

plantings
in a botanic garden
distant harmony

an ark
in the arboretum
the freedom
of a new home
hidden history

Halloween Night

flicker
in triangle eyes
pumpkin moon

there must be
good and bad gods. . .
light
on the mountain trail
Ryōkan moon

forest canopy
outsmarting the trickster
moon

who is hiding
in my cat's eye
watching me—
the moon
framed green

trick or treat
a couple of ghosts
in the moonlight

welcome home
a cup of hot wine
with cinnamon. . .
sticking moon
on top of a witch tower

Note:
Ryōkan moon: references this tanka by Zen monk & poet, Ryōkan 1758 –
1831, translated by Mariko Kitakubo

wait for
the moon light
to go back home
mountain trail has
many chestnut prickles

After the Argument

little frogs
splashing in the water
day's end

my tears
uncontrolled
spill and spill
only the lurid sunset
understands

The Wide Sky

longing. . .
the wide sky
of Okinawa
a sugarcane straw
at the café, Ginza

sipping water
a dolphin's lethal grazing
at the bottle island

hope
or hopeless
can we
return to the shore
aimless waves

sea boulders
splashed by the froth
cormorants

the amniotic fluid
of Mother Ocean
let's sing
the deep tide song
with coelacanths

open seas
a juvenile humpback whale
flips its tail

Testing the Limits

we are
tiny beings
still here
on this windy earth
Mother planet

sonic boom
rattling my windows
returning spacecraft

gathering
in the crater
formed
by shock waves
nuclear test

a piece of space junk
on the ocean floor
gravity

eternal stream
of the Milky Way
where
did our tears come from
and where will they go

the deafening roar
of Niagara
water ice on Mars

a city's landmarks

From 32,000 Feet

sleeping
Scandinavian
peninsula
under midnight sun,
Arctic Ocean route

drowsy in my seat
the flight attendant
serves ice cream

lime sherbet
with champagne
where will
drift ice go. . .
under Polaris

endless blues
alone with three hundred
other passengers

tilting
the right wing
to escape
from turbulence
in our lives

a city's landmarks
growing larger
prayers for peace

Jet Stream

empty skies
and yet, somewhere. . .
your plane

reverberation
between Leo
and Libra
floating without
nationality

Asakusa

tourists pose
by the thunder gate
jinriki-sha

cherry petals
were dancing
at Senso-ji
together in the photo
us with incense smoke

red-faced in the wind
of a spring day
paper lantern

a couple
of Nioh watches us
since we visited
sweet rain
of Asakusa

my last package
of matcha sweet treats
empty suitcases

am I
mishearing?
happy liveliness
from that April
pale blue sky

Note:
jinriki-sha: Japanese rickshaw
Senso-ji: Ancient Buddhist temple in the Asakusa area of Tokyo. It is Tokyo's
oldest temple.
Nioh: Guardian temple statues which protect the temple from evil spirits.

The Queen Mary

seagulls
a little girl watches
the ship sail in

father's hand
was big and warm
before
my story begins
scent of the beach

live band on board
dancing cheek to cheek
at the high school prom

toasting
the fruit punch
our poetry
is still in the wind
string quartet

horn blast
a hundred fifty poets
on deck

that
antique smell. . .
I meet
an elegant ghost
at the end of the corridor

Meiji Jingu

sun on the water
an egret meditates
in the shrine garden

making
shining circles
around us
like waterfowl,
our thankful prayer

I write my heart
too soon for irises
in the inner garden

the leaf
looks like a sword ...
shōbu iris
please don't bring us
another war

crossing the bridge
I am lost
in the forest

how many Torii
did I go thorough?
hopefully
the next gate
will be welcoming

Note:
Torii: A traditional Japanese gate often at the entrance or within a Shinto
shrine, marking the transition from the mundane to the sacred.

The Getty

autumn shapes
the tram's hillside path
from the parking lot

bird of paradise
by the fence
we smiled. . .
before covid 19,
before military invasion

no Peace rose
cactus gardens
on the museum roof

thorny shadows
on the wall
there was
an orange stain
shaped heart

writing our story
illustrated manuscripts
on display

separation
brings us
closer
the smoothness
of driftwood

Inokashira Park

empty swan boats
cherry blossoms
floating

whiteness
of the new canvas
blank
to paint our time
spring again

morning sun
sparkles on the lake
ducks gather

soon
they will fly to
Kamchatka
skies and water
waterfowl

cloud cover
we cross the bridge
into silence

tell me
your folklore
newborn water
hidden spring
in the park

Midnight in Los Angeles

all-night diner
menu flip between
burgers and breakfast

under
the white half moon
16 hours ahead
Ume Shu
for your aperitif

Note:
Ume Shu: Plum sake

Beyond the Marine Layer

an ocean of traffic
far below the sugar pine
island in the sky

here was
the seabed,
long ago...
Himalayan poppy
unforgettable blue

Governor's Island

old prison
the view of Liberty
and her torch

hollow eyes. . .
his childhood
hopefully
speaks of love
Buttermilk Channel

an island
in a sea of strangers
carry-on bag

rhythm
of the lighthouse
under
star ice—
a journey in years

city sparkle
a short ferry ride
to a different world

long wait
on the midnight pier
darkness
in the ancient stream
departure to freedom

Note:
Buttermilk Channel: Small tidal strait in Upper New York Bay in
New York City

Cancelled Flights

tiny
reflection
of the airplane
where will you go
in a glass of Merlot?

stranded
at the airport
a second glass

as the road bends

Passageway

stagnated
in the long tunnel
without
stars, birds
and voices

headlights on
yearning for a glimpse
of forests

chant
of the Gemini
our hope
was born
from the dark

underpass graffiti
a toddler asleep
in the shopping cart

sky blue
message memo
to heaven
chalk powder
in the arcade

we honk our horn
as the road bends. . .
whiff of ocean

Maple Avenue

winter wind
the last leaf
in my driveway

what can I bake
for my friend
his desire
to disappear. . .
bonfire sunset

Remembrance

the terrace
bordered with
poinsettia
a cup of coffee
for each life

soft snow
the names still listed
in my phone

Idyllic

time to sit
with summer roses
aphids

is it a dream
Monet's garden
in Giverny
afterglow of fireflies
before bitterness

Ninth Month

apple orchard
waiting for the first
hints of red

grass path
to the woody gate
release
or protect
unborn fluff

First Blanket

behind
pale cloud lace
the dignity
before perfection
chestnut moon

waiting, waiting
the slow rise
of the sun

previously. . .
what do you
remember?
smiles for the sky
newborn baby

first blanket
your face peeking out
from its folds

The Color Red

a fir tree
in the maple forest
forever
green. . .
melancholy

dressing up drab clothes
with Christmas bling
I feel like singing

Lego Box

tiny pieces
become
our world. . .
picking up only
innocent elements

kaleidoscopes
of brightly colored pieces
Starry Night *in 3-D*

passion
of the vortex
still there
in the deep sky
Vincent Van Gogh

swirling blocks
in circular patterns
childhood artist

release
from a spiral
labyrinth
a flying ladybird
summer morning

follow
the yellow brick road
Lego box

Coming of Age

angel hair pasta
her baby tooth
beneath a pillow

first kiss
under the olive tree,
garden party
on this mellow
summer solstice

Following the Strands

glamour
of nocturnal
salt water
born from a moon
in Andromeda

expanse
of the universe
a boy and his dog

journey
of the double helix
has no ending. . .
ancient dragonfly shadows
by the stream

tar pit
on Wilshire Boulevard
saber-toothed tiger

iridescent tail
of a baby lizard
Goddess Nyx
gives him wings
sherbet moon

the speed of sound
through water
whale song

Opening the Door

first
snowy night
I can't hide
inside of me anymore
popcorn popping

Christmas cardinal
I paint my nails
red

Sunday in June

which color
did he like. . .
hydrangea?
abandoned again
each Father's Day

shining light
from a mother sun
crescent moon smile

my words drift

Panta Rhei

from the cliff
throwing myself
to escape. . .
I drift away in
a seaglass bottle

my words drift
for miles and miles. . .
will they reach your shore?

after
the sleepless night. . .
at the beach,
a brilliant cut of
the diamond message

exposed tidepools
an ochre sea star clings
to the rock

without
predators
a baby crab
relaxes at the corner
of the throne

perfect worlds. . .
each one disappears
with incoming waves

Note:
Panta Rhei: "Everything flows," a concept in the philosophy of Heraclitus

A Cappella

mallards
can you see
sunshine??
longing . . .
under the thick clouds

my dreams fly
a mountain pokes through
the mist

seeing me
in your world
please
find yourself
in matching sunglasses

backyard pond
I hear your words
in the mirror

finding
one wing of
a pair. . .
we each sing
a different verse

a cappella
at midnight
moonglow

9th Inning

losing streak
the crack as his bat
hits a foul ball

every motion
stops and restarts
slowly. . .
we catch our breath
Gyakuten Sayonara!

<u>Note:</u>
Gyakuten Sayonara: "Coming from behind," a "good bye" hit, i.e. a home run
with bases loaded when your team is behind and is now ahead!

The Empty House

autumn leaves
nursery rhymes echo
in my head

fingerprints
left on the sky
where are
the missing
children

empty room
a floppy stuffed
bunny

you are wind
blowing away
the world sings
your song
around me always

Weathering the Storm

severe
thunderstorm
I want to
go back to childhood
protected days

afraid of lightning
snaking down
two sisters together

Mother Angel

dust
on a Tiffany lamp
estate sale

through
the antique glass
dawn
comes into
the world

Through the Clouds

wiping off
and wiping off
the dark. . .
footsteps
in the cloud

foggy morning
searching for a ray of light
within the gray

I can't see
my fairy shoes
in the weeds
trapped by gravity
within the haze

blurry-eyed
a bee dusts
the pollen

loving
your crossed
fingers...
a bottle of mead
across the ocean

outstretched wings
the scan beep
of a boarding pass

Garden Music

silent blooms
in a camellia forest
pond ripples

scarlet
tsubaki flower
fringed white
aria
under the moonbow

Note
Tsubaki: camellia

Unfinished Dream

dizziness
of purple scent
the new born
dead branch
mysterious wisteria

blooms droop
from the eaves
my heavy eyelids

clusters
are growing
for tomorrow
thinking about
Shiki's later days

the rain
in our lives
lavender plumes

the blur
of a mellow
shower. . .
unknown future
unfinished dream

the sun peeks out
for a moment
rainbow bridge

Focus

an egret wading
its distorted image
in the ripples

so tired
the stranger must
have had hard times
is that me in the mirror
at the platform?

Wings

milkweed in bloom
a caterpillar hidden
under a leaf

who can
recognize me
the joy
or loss—
metamorphosis

Publication Credits

9th Inning, *right hand pointing* #151, April 2023
A Cappella, *Kokako*, #34, Spring 2021
Asakusa, *Dashboard Horus*, 7/21/2022
Beach in Malaysia, *Shot Glass Journal*, #39, January 2023
Both Sides of the Ocean, *Kokako*, #33, Autumn 2020
Coming of Age, *#FemkuMag*, Issue 34, November 2022
Distance 2020, *Under the Basho*, 2020
Ebb and Flow, *Failed Haiku*, July 2022
Footsteps, *right hand pointing* #151, April 2023
Forecast, *Shot Glass Journal*, #39, January 2023
Forest Bathing, *Scarlet Dragonfly Journal*, 7/12/2022
Hanging Overhead, *Failed Haiku*, July 2022
Inokashira Park, *Kokako* #36, Spring 2022
Lego Box, *Scarlet Dragonfly Journal*, 5/26/2022
Meiji Jingu, *Dashboard Horus,* 7/21/2022
Motherless, *right hand pointing* #151, April 2023
Resolve, *Scarlet Dragonfly Journal*, 2/21/2023
Seedlings, *Under the Basho*, 2022
Sirius Rising, *right hand pointing* #151, April 2023
Stormy, *Frameless Sky* #16, 2022
The Color Red, *Scarlet Dragonfly Journal*, 12/25/2022
The Queen Mary, *California Quarterly 48.4*, Winter 2022
Through the Clouds, (Published as "Uncertain"), *Under the Basho*, 2022
Under the Sun, *Scarlet Dragonfly Journal*, 6/23/2022
Wings, *Shot Glass Journal* #39, January 2023

CPSIA information can be obtained
at www.ICGtesting.com
Printed in the USA
LVHW031412100423
743966LV00004B/280